gallery guide

GOYA
Black Paintings

gallery guide

GOYA
Black Paintings

Valeriano Bozal

Fundación Amigos del Museo del Prado

FLOOR PLAN OF THE PRADO MUSEUM

SECOND FLOOR

FIRST FLOOR

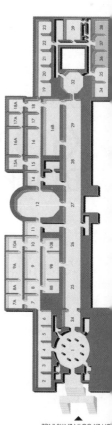

UPPER GOYA ENTRANCE

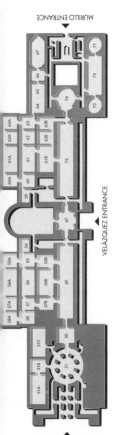

MURILLO ENTRANCE

67 66 65 64 74 73 72 71

63A 63B 62B 61B 75

62A 62 61A 61 60A 60 59

47 VELÁZQUEZ ENTRANCE

57A 56A 55A 54 55 56 57B 56B 55B 49 58B

58A 58 57

51C 50

51B 51A 51

LOWER GOYA ENTRANCE

100 101 102

BASEMENT

© Publication: Fundación Amigos del Museo del Prado
© Texts: Valeriano Bozal, 2003
© Images: Museo Nacional del Prado

Layout: Marta Ruifernández
Axonometric projections: Ana Pazó Espinosa
Edition: Tf. Editores
Printed in Tf. Artes Gráficas, S. A. Alcobendas (Madrid)

  ISBN: 84-95452-19-7
  D. L.: M-51271-2003

Cover: Goya, *Asmodea* (detail), Museo Nacional del Prado, Madrid

Fifth edition: December 2003

Introduction

The *Black Paintings* is the name given to that series of oils that Goya painted directly onto the walls of two of the rooms of his country house between 1819/20 and 1823 and that by which they have come to be known, albeit this overall title for them can only be authenticated for the 20th Century. Whether or not they were previously so called, we do not know. Of all Goya's works, these have, perhaps, the most immediate impact for us and this not only for the nature of their subject matter or the sombre, blackened and overpowering way in which this is conveyed but as much again for their starkly arresting visual punch and the power of their expressivity to button hole our responses across the ages. These are no commissioned stuff, in these works Goya bowed to no one's taste but his own and so put down his thoughts on Man's estate and the World. His influence upon contemporary Expressionism and Surrealism has been gigantic and his delineating of things absurd, violent and irrational has become a model that bestrides modern culture. The paintings come from two rooms of similar size but differing layout, one upstairs, the other down, in the house bought by the artist in 1819 and which he left to his grandson in 1823 when he was driven away to France. The meaning of the works has been the subject of much lively debate and as yet there is no general agreement among the various schools as to the same and so it would be as well to have all the facts to hand before making a go at an explanation of them.

The first fact is Goya's buying his country house, *La Quinta del Sordo* ("The Deaf Man's Place"). Why he bought an out of town house – close to the present day Paseo de Extremadura – and made it his permanent residence can be explained in the light of various factors and the first of these must be political. After the Peninsular War, the restored King Ferdinand VII let lose an absolutist repression upon Madrid life and especially against any such who, like Goya, had had pro-french or liberal friends and were thus seen askance by the Inquisition. Then personal considerations must be borne in mind, the artists' age, his poor health and even, perhaps, the affair he might have been having with Leocadia Zorrilla, not to mention, though we must, the taste he had acquired for comfortable middle class living for which the new house made a very worthy setting. Professionally, there is the fact that Goya had been gradually easing up on his activity as Painter to the Royal Household, his obligations here being met, more and more, by Vicente López. This is by no means to say that Goya renounced his post as the kings painter however, for he held on to this even after his flight to France.

These self same factors also serve to allow for a discussion of the drives that gave rise to the works themselves, for they are shot through with a sharp disdain for institutions like the Inquisition, scorn both violence and empty habit, are soaked in an overall air of airlessness and gloom, an air that echoes the toll of the painter's aging and recurrent illness – which went through a turn for the worse in late 1819 – as it does his state of mind and of heart. Pictures he would have found it hard to have done had he been fully busied with fulfilling his duties as Painter Royal. Be all this as it might be, it is as true that the tremendous physical out-pouring that the *Black Paintings* represent is not commonly found among the depressed. His scorn for the Inquisition is against a body formally abolished in March 1820 in a moment of hope for the liberals who had made Ferdinand VII submit to swearing the Constitution of 1812. To this must be added the fact that the works were conceived as "General (pictorial) Reflexions" and not as representing any concrete or special events. This leads me to think of the *Black Paintings* as being the outcome of a process of drawing overall conclusions or summing up both from the political march of events and the artist's private and professional experiences and, as such, of them as not being tied in with giving shape to things specific but rather as representing new insights into a world seen as essentially tragic.

The *Black Paintings* as a Composite Creation

Goya painted fourteen oils in all directly on to the walls of two rooms, rooms which measured 9.02 x 4.51 metres and differed as to the surfaces available. In each of the side walls of the lower room there were two gaps that thus imposed a broad horizontal composition between them, whereas in the upper room, there being but one gap, two compositions, likewise horizontal though smaller, were called for. The remaining, vertical format works were done on either side of the rooms' doors. The original placing of each work has long taxed the historian, as this is seen as being one of the keys to the overall development of images undertaken by the artist.

They were executed between 1819/20 and 1823 and their existence was attested by Antonio Brugada in his inventory of the effects made on the painter's death (1828). They stayed where they were but none too well looked after until the last owner of the house, Baron F. E. d'Erlanger called in Salvador Martínez Cubells, the then restorer to the Prado Museum, to lift them and re-back them on canvas in 1874. After being shown at the Paris World Fair of 1878, they were made over to the state in 1881 and thus came to us at the Prado Museum.

Transferring them to canvas entailed changes in their size, some damage, some touching up and re-painting despite which the works were not robbed of their aesthetic impact nor their power of suggestion. X-ray study has revealed that they are painted over other, unfinished, works that were in the main, brighter landscape studies with small figures much more in keeping with the decoration for a country house. When he painted these nor why he painted them over or out is, likewise, unknown to us as if why he at times retained parts of them at others obliterated them altogether or why he always altered their mood. Some idea of them can be had from the background landscape to *The Single Stick Duel* and the left background to *The Holy Office's Walk* the artist in both cases here leaving in part of his first work as valid.

It should always be remembered that these are a linked series of works, a whole, and that there is much relevant interplay between them. An attempt is here made to insist upon where they originally stood as to each other and in which of the two rooms they did so for this has much to offer towards both an understanding and an appreciation of them.

- Ground floor room: *Saturn, Judith and Holofernes, A Manola: Leocadia Zorrilla, Two Old People, Two Old People Eating, Sabbath (The Great He-Goat), Saint Isidro's Pilgrimage.*
- Upper floor room: *Two Women and a Man, The Reading, The Single Stick Duel, The Holy Office's Walk, The Fates (Atropos), Asmodea, A Drowning Dog.*

Historians have never come to any agreement about the subject matter of some of the pictures and it would be odd if the visitor were not to find them puzzling. To guide the visitor, to guide another's eye is then but to help it find out for itself a possible "why" these works are as they are, to suggest a "what", and point out things worthy of attention. There works are open-ended images and though hermetic in much, in much else amazingly immediate. No guide can either see for the visitor not react in his stead. But he can ask him to stay, to stare – and not to run away.

THE GROUND FLOOR ROOM

Saturn

Judith and Holofernes

A Manola: Leocadia Zorrilla

Two Old People

Two Old People Eating

Sabbath (The Great He-Goat)

Saint Isidro's Pilgrimage

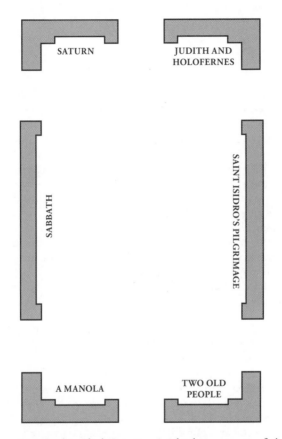

SATURN

JUDITH AND HOLOFERNES

SABBATH

SAINT ISIDRO'S PILGRIMAGE

A MANOLA

TWO OLD PEOPLE

Layout the *Black Paintings* in the lower room of the country house beside the river Manzanares

Saturn (cat. 763)
143 x 81 cm

Also known as *Saturn Devouring one of his Children,*
this work is of key importance for the understanding of
the ground floor as a whole. Goya here gives us an often
engraved and much painted subject of engraving. Saturn,
Cronus, Time is a mythological archetype to be found in
Hesiod's *Theogony*: son of Gea, Mother Earth, he castrates
his father, Uranus, with a flint sickle given to him by his
mother, the blood flowing from the wound – besides
fertilizing the World – brings into being the Erinnyes or
Furies, the Giants or Titans and the Nymphs. Later
Saturn, now wed to his sister Rhea, devours their off-
spring as soon as they are born but their mother manages
to cunningly save the youngest, Zeus who, once come to
manhood, compels his sire to regurgitate his brood and
then undertakes a victorious war against the blood-sprung
Giants or Titans. Saturn has justly become seen as the
presiding mythological deity of Death and Time, Old Age
and Melancholy and of Drought, the genius of War,
Dearth and Catastrophes.

The moment in the tale that has most often seized the
artistic imagination is that in which Saturn devours his
children. A good example of this is P. P. Rubens *Saturn* (cat.
1678) in the Prado's own collection, a work possibly
known to Goya himself. The visitor could do worse than
take a brief look at both works, the better to appreciate how
very differently these two giants understood the scene.

16

Rubens, *Saturn* (cat. 1678)

Rubens goes along with traditional iconography and gives us an ancient Saturn who, clasping a scythe in his right hand and sat upon clouds in a cosmic landscape, is busy at bolting down a little boy. Goya gives us none of this, makes no hint at where the action is taking place, does away with the prop scythe and even the victim is no longer a loveable wee child. The victim, as it has its back to the viewer and is headless, we know no more about than that it is adult, young and, by its buttocks, thighs and legs, more likely a woman than a man.

Goya, though he has no truck with its mythological trappings, makes all the more of the cruelty of the scene which he raises to the heights of paroxysm: Old Saturn's eyes bulge, his maw drools, his hands mangle at a corpse more fit for a shambles all of which underscores the terrible humanness of the scene. The close night, the light that plays upon the victim (female?) and the god's visage, the gory red, the inertia of the cadaver as against the ancient's excitement, all highlight the scene's blatantly negative charge. There is nothing here of Melancholy nor even Death, here is the loathsome cruelty that an old man might exercise upon a young woman.

Goya's trick of deforming the human body, its movements and limbs to create an impression of latent bestiality can be found in the work of such present day painters as the Dublin born englishman Francis Bacon. The blatant and uncompromising visual stamp of the images, the rank gloominess of the anecdote, the unashamed pictorial fact of the figures and the lack of all narrative packaging to the whole are what make this expressive scene modern – just that.

Judith and Holofernes (cat. 764)

143 x 81 cm

This painting forms a pair with *Saturn* though here the tale runs vice-versa and a woman it is who kills a man. The title refers to a biblical scene (Judith, 13), in which Judith lops off the head of Holofernes. As in *Saturn*, Goya makes nothing of the setting and goes, head down, for the action: here we see the sweep of the arm with the sword, the gesture and stance of the woman, that of the procuress-like servant while the severed head in the bottom right hand corner all but goes unnoticed.

The lighting makes great play of Judith's femininity, her physical presence, her naked bust and arms, her modern seeming headdress. Goya needs none of the jewels nor rich dress that the biblical tale refers to. The setting for the scene – the interior of Holofernes' tent – is given the sketchiest treatment – just a dark backdrop with neither hangings nor other furnishings that might fix it. The woman's violent act, its cruel energy are what the attention focuses upon and focused, it cannot do other than see the act as being very like so many others as violent in sort that Goya had brought the eye to in his times such as those he had witnessed in the Peninsular War or during the absolutist reaction that followed in its wake. But yet again, Goya's mastery of his theme is shown by the lack here of any anecdotal fixing detail, an absence that thus lends his image a universal, nonparochial impact.

A Manola*: Leocadia Zorrilla (cat. 754)

145 x 129 cm

A female figure rests against a funerary mound. The painting stood across from *Saturn* and *Judith and Holofernes* and would have seemed to contemplate them. The Manola's pose corresponds to the established mode of depicting Melancholy. Much ink has been spilt upon who this woman was and it is thought that she was Leocadia Zorrilla, wife to Isidoro Weiss, though what she meant to the painter still remains rather cloudy. We do know that she lived with Goya in his house and went along with him to Bordeaux. and that the then aged painter doted upon Rosario, Leocadia's daughter, so much so that there have been some historians that have been led to believe that she could well have been his own natural daughter. Be she Leocadia or not – and the figure shown seems younger than Leocadia who was already 32 in 1820 – the picture is not so much a portrait as an allegory that turns upon the veiled beauty of the Manola and the funerary mound. Her thoughtful gaze does not quite lift the eye from her slim and supple body, her generous bust or those ever so tiny feet... The open background is in contrast with focal grouping and is, with its blues and clouds, amongst the happiest of Goya's output. Here the overall tone is not brooding though the foreground group is solemn.

---

*Fashionable Madrid society took to aping the styles and manners of the city's demi-mondains, male and female, in Goya's times and far some time later. See Richard Ford, *Handbook for Spain*, 1846. *(Tr. N.)*

Two Old People (cat. 759)

142 x 65 cm

Companion to (the) *Leocadia*, situated on the other side of the entrance, Goya has painted a bearded old man, propping himself up with a staff and wrapped in a cape, being whispered at by a deformed figure. The only hint of what is going on is given by the contrast between the two figures. The elderly bearded man, both in his face and gesture, bears a stamp of dignity, a quality not to be found in the whisperer with his beastly maw, brow wrinkling up across his skull and what would appear to be huge and pointed ears. The jangler has many of the traits of a fiend and to that fraternity could well belong. Goya often drew such figures. While his hand was great at portraying the young, especially young women, so it was with the aged as well. If the young breath their sensuality and erotic being, the aged are all ambiguity, have sunk into a time of deformity, have lost any charm they might once have had and are left with naught but a dignity, like that of the bearded fellow, to lend their lives something positive. If the fiend is intimating the old man's end to him, the ancient at least can bear the new with serenity.

Maybe it would be going to far to see a kind of metaphoric self-portrait of Goya himself in the good old man but then again the fact is that he was old – 74 in 1820 – and had already heard his call given more than once.

25

Two Old People Eating (cat. 762)
49 x 83 cm

It is not known exactly where this picture stood. Both its size and format would seem to argue for over one of the doors so it could well have figured over the entrance to the downstairs room. However, certain technical considerations might lead to its being understood as having been done for the upstairs room. There is little to no agreement as to its content either. Only one of the old people holds a spoon and is about to eat and what is more, looks more like an old woman than a man. The other figure pointing at her (?) side looks like an eyeless corpse and could well be an image of Death itself.

The subject is as hermetic as the work is simple and Goya's skill when giving us a powerful yet enigmatic subject is here once again amazing. The crone's gaze, the wicked grin on the gummy mouth, the over-pronounced chin are echoed in the acolyte. What this second creature is pointing at is anybody's guess. Are they papers they have before them, a list perhaps? Is the fate of those on it being whispered about to the grinning hag? As so often in this master's work, what is suggested or could be supposed swamps mere certainty.

These creatures are at one with the cast of witches and crones with which Goya peoples so many of his drawings, plates and paintings and blend into the subject matter of many other of the *Black Paintings*. Rather than reflecting the World as it is, they, through allegory, do so as it is sensed to be. Those who dwell within this world of shades and expressive dramatic effects are emblematic of the paintings proper to this room.

The counterpoint here between the genre nature of the work's motif and Goya's treatment of the same is not only eye catching but most disturbing. By rights, we should be enjoying the most domestic of scenes but the way in which the sharp old hag is expressed has blighted this expected pleasure, has so fractured it as to turn it inside out. This shattering of conventional expectations is a constant throughout the whole gamut of the *Black Paintings* where everyday subjects are given, time and again, darkly tragic overtones. Even the apparently mythological reference of some of the scenes is peeled away by Goya who draws our attention rather to the alarmingly come-day-go-day realities that tie in with his "high" subject matter.

Despite its size – it is the smallest of the *Black Paint-ings* –, *Two Old People Eating* is a most striking work, its skull-like faces being charged not only with irony but stamped, withal, with a most sarcastic grimace by which the artist breathes a horrid sort of liveliness into what, otherwise, would be little more than two warmed-up death masks.

Sabbath (The Great He-Goat) (cat. 761)
140 x 435 cm

From the left hand side wall of the lower room, this is the only *Black Painting* that had no neighbours. Goya has here used a freehanded brush stroke that has followed the pure gesture of his wrist and hand as if a broad house painter's stroke were aimed at, this giving the work dynamism and lending rhythm and direction to the faces of the assembled witches crowding before a devil in hegoat's shape who presides over the rite assisted by a secretary/curate to his right. Set apart, a young woman, still almost a child, awaits her initiation sat upon a chair.

The mob of witches that are the focus of the scene is not caught in motion and yet is not still, being fanned alive by the brush work, its stroke and the composition endowing the mass with a terrible mute dynamism as though all were fired by a dreadful ecstasy. The faces in it are deformed, the bodies doubled up or over, some show fear. If they are closely examined, different types of folk can be made out, for, though most are witches, there is a friar just in front of the "curate" and a working man or farm hand in the third head from the far left. These character sketches do not, however, disturb the mass vortex feel of the whole, a feat that marks out Goya from the rest of the painters of his times.

Cat. 761 (detail)

The setting is left vague. Certain objects and foreground references would seem to bespeak somewhere out-of-doors but what then of the close atmospheric darkness that crowds the left and upper background? We are thus within a metaphor for the world, and "metaphoric" is the sense of Life that the child woman is about to learn of, as her initiation will be into things deathly. Goya here returns to a subject matter that had exercised his imagination at the tail end of the 18th Century in drawings, plates and paintings, but now there is no comic touch or even critical tone. He does not here attack witchcraft or even mock it, he but shows Night's own world. The crowding witches and their like, the

Cat. 761 (detail)

presiding and overbearing male goat, its being contrasted with the maiden, are all dramatic stratagems that the circular "spin" of the composition further heightens.

Be it formally, iconographically or semantically, Goya's works are in many ways heralds of many aspect of modern art. His pictorial approach, visual punch, the expressivity of a brush work that at times seems downright gestural, the ease with which he shapes the irrational, the deformity and weird sea changes in his figures are all still to be found as novelties in the art and culture of our own times.

*Saint Isidro's Pilgrimage** (cat. 760)

138 x 436 cm

This painting must bring to mind those paintings Goya did in the 18th Century of public holidays and events, especially the one he drew up as a cartoon for a tapestry never, alas, realized, on the subject of the *Meadow of Saint Isidro*. The sense of fun of those images, their luminosity and chromatic play, the lively manners of their protagonist, the very concrete expressing of just where all was taking place are here absent... gone and this is a very different world. Now shades shroud this procession of celebrants who come on towards the Viewer. Their music, if there were any, would be sodden with tragedy and hopelessness rather than bright with joy. Even the veiled

beauty of the women behind their "mantillas" is drowned in the squalor of the group.

And whatever charm that the setting might once have had – and indeed the landscape that Goya suggests and even some of the figures could be attractive – is drained of all promise by the character of this so unpromising rout.

The scene has been understood by some historians as a *Saturnalia*, a festival in honour of Saturn who, like Saint Isidro, was a patron of labourers. This could indeed be what this outing celebrates but here there is nothing of the excess and merry making of the classical festival. Goya's painting does not bespeak the past as would a work redolent of nostalgia for classical mythology but rather is cheek to jowl with a deadeningly humdrum present. The characters, their dress, their very standing are all of Goya's

Cat. 760 (detail)

own times or even less determined than that. The master
here is in no way after a historical reconstruction – any
more than he is any other of the *Black Paintings* – and if he
does hint at classical iconography, he does so only to
underline his present world of the turn of the century.

They are a mixed bunch that are coming towards us.
There are beggars, workingmen, fieldhands, the well-
heeled and the comfortably off, people from every call and
calling in life, for all qualities and stations of people took
part in this celebration, as we do too, for, willy-nilly, he also
sweeps us up into the picture which not only spills towards
us but, by the stares and glances of some of the foreground
figures, draws us into its action and scope by the eye
language dialogue that these stares and glances provoke.

This last is a thing common to the whole run of *Black
Paintings*. Goya does not offer here material to be looked

34

Cat. 760 (detail)

upon from without but has cunningly made use of elements in his composition that strike up an immediate affinity between the world of his works and that of his spectators. A virtual conversation is thus established between the viewer and the foreground beggars in the procession. Their movement into the Viewers territory, their presence, stares and gestures beg this of him, beseech it, mutely impose it.

The technical elements Goya uses to achieve these effects are wonderfully plastic. The group crowds out the foreground and makes itself the focal line to such a degree that the sheer weight of its density of feeling, its ill-defined dimensions, that left unseen, that which might be – or be coming – behind it quite unsettles the spectator and, this riveted, the eye clings to what can be accomodated and simply seen: the celebrants themselves.

*A "romería", far from being a formal pilgrimage, was more a local day off and general outing to the saint in question's shrine. *(Tr. N.)*

THE UPPER FLOOR ROOM

Two Women and a Man
The Reading
The Single Stick Duel
The Holy Office's Walk
The Fates (Atropos)
Asmodea
A Drowning Dog

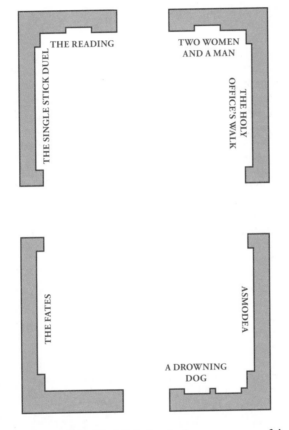

THE READING

TWO WOMEN
AND A MAN

THE SINGLE STICK DUEL

THE HOLY
OFFICE'S WALK

THE FATES

ASMODEA

A DROWNING
DOG

Layout of the *Black Paintings* in the upper room of the country house beside the river Manzanares

Two Women and a Man (cat. 765)

125 x 66 cm

A visitor coming into the upper room of the *Quinta* would have been met by two paintings one on either side of the door: *Two Women and a Man* and *The Reading*. Both, like their neighbouring horizontal works, would seem very different in their subject matter to those to be seen in the lower room. Now the mundane rules, even the frankly vulgar, as if we were faced again with a new set of "very common commonplace scenes".

The poses and gestures of the man and both women have always given rise to much comment and as much – and contradictory – interpretation. At present it is generally held that the composition is about masturbation: the man in masturbating and the watching women are laughing either at him or with him. There is, however, no hint here of any comment at all on this, let alone censure.

They could be in some kind of interior or, then again, outside and maybe even in the street. Once again, Goya cheats us out of our certainties. The light falls on the arm, the elbow, the white shirt of the man and some onto the lap of one of the women slightly to the rear of him. Shadow swallows all else, deepening the further we travel from the lighted focal point. In this way and although the scene has nothing biblical nor mythological to it, it has its affinities with the scenes in the room below and with the others on this floor.

This similarity also extends to the characters depicted here. The man's ecstatic gesture is yet another instance of that grotesque twisting into the bestial of other figures in

Cat. 765 (detail)

Goya's work, the giggling woman would be quite at home at a Sabbath of the lower room, even though she seems younger than those witches; while the other, to the left, has very much in common with Judith's handmaid.

These affinities can lead to two ways of understanding the picture, there being those who, thanks to them, argue that it should be seen as another allegory as the subject of onanism lends itself to such a treatment while others – and myself among them – while in no way denying this possibility, would tend to see it in quite another light, rather seeing the historical scenes as being shot through with that same everyday hardness that here is the dominant note. *Two Women and a Man* offers no bolt hole

Cat. 765 (detail)

from the here and now and this ties in very well with Goya's methods of working when he puts aside all mythological and biblical trappings.

The artist has nailed his eye upon the expression proper to each one of his subjects. The gross delight in the man's face marked by his drooling gawp and leery eyes are contrasted with the brutal guffaw of the woman watching him and the pert glance of the woman to the left. All three together set up an interplay of reactions around the act that, though patent, is never spelt out, all of which lends the icon a hermetic reek itself born as much of the painter's indifference to the act as such as his abounding interest in the reactions of his protagonists' to it.

The Reading (cat. 766)

125 x 65 cm

The publishing of newspapers, pamphlets and all manner of other productions, especially if satirical or political, hit a peak during the three years of liberal government *(El Trienio Liberal)* thanks to its granting of freedom to the press. People read alone or quite often in groups like that Goya gives us here where we have a gathering of men to listen to a group reading of one of these broadsheets. Whether this paper is a political one or not, we cannot tell from the picture alone, any more than we can make out exactly where the reading is taking place – they tended to be held in cafes, the street or private parlours. Yet again Goya has left us in the dark on this part of his subject matters.

The lighting of the scene, like that of *Two Women and a Man,* seeks an expressive rather than a natural effect. Playing on group centre, it has no given source and scatters shadows in every direction. Thus, and so simply, Goya turns what could well have been another's everyday and picturesque scene – and so it was treated in many prints and cartoons – into a dramatic event. The picture's charged atmosphere is its dominant key and highlights both characters and their very limited gestures. What Goya homes us in on is thus their absorbed attentiveness and this is almost as intense as our own. The spectator's curiosity is so very much a parallel to that of these listener-spectators that, as spell bound as they are, being drawn into the world of the work is all but inevitable.

43

The Single Stick Duel (cat. 758)
125 x 261 cm

This is one of the best and most widely known of the *Black Paintings*. It shows a brutal duel to the death in which the duellists, buried up to the knee, are denied all option to flee. Though no one can have any doubt as to what is going on, nobody could see the work as a mere anecdote. It is as much an allegory upon the violence of Spanish life in the painter's times, time's overloaded with conflict, as it is a comment upon the congenital violence of his nation at all times and his fellow countrymen's dreadful tendency towards fraternal strife that so marks them out.

The image can be as broadly or narrowly understood as the viewer chooses but whatever the choice, the scene is as sure to imprint itself on the memory in one way or another with all its tragic drama, plead against the inescapable fate to which the combatants are condemned and scorch the mind's retina with the extreme violence with which its overbearing all is expressed and do all this with all the simplicity of a blow to the face.

This is one of the few works in the *Black Paintings* series that darkness does not dominate. The landscape is bright and clear, the fields and hills that spread to the skyline offer an almost bucolic setting, highlighted by the blue of the sky, the fair clouds and the strength of the sunlight. This peaceful beauty only intensifies the scene's dramatic impact and makes the more explicit the harshness of the world of men as against that of the gently browsing cattle of the middle ground.

The luminous background landscape has been left in from the previous, underlying painting. It shows us two things of which the most obvious must be that the original paintings that Goya intended for his walls had nothing tragic about them but were very much more the sort of work then thought suitable for decorating a country house than the *Black Paintings* could ever have been accepted as

Cat. 758 (detail)

being. Second only to this, it shows the painter's original work for the wall to have been by a hand in total control of the ways and means of his art, up to creating landscapes of breath-taking beauty well beyond the pastoral bucolics that had crowded up the walls of his age. Goya uses, above all, light and air as the "ingredients" for his composition thus modulating the luminosity of the scene and making its atmospheric density the unifying chord to its all. Thus the two men locked in brutal combat are seen in silhouette. By the use of such simplicity of means when giving body to his images he lends them an added value and meaning out and beyond any mere representing them be it ever so formally. The stand point for both landscape and background is not the same as that for the figures, the comfortable distancing of the first thus further throwing the fighters almost into the viewer's/spectator's own limits of "safe" space.

The Holy Office's Walk (cat. 755)
127 x 263 cm

Also known as *Pilgrimage to Saint Isidro's Spring* this picture stood across from the previous one, *The Single Stick Duel*, and bears some resemblances to it. As before, the master has kept in a good part of his original, half painted over, first work – the landscape and some small figures – but has given the whole a new twist that has little to do with the mood of his earlier effort.

Goya gives us a procession that would appear to be led by a toady of the Holy Office who is the right foreground figure with a fool's face and gestures and all decked out in out-dated garb. He is surrounded by a court of hags and besoms that are in no wise the superiors of the witches in the *Sabbath* or the crones of his drawings and engravings. The same goes for those coming in from the right, some of whom, crippled or deformed, stagger along on crutches or with sticks. The pilgrims seek a cure for these misfortunes but Goya's foreground figures would seem to offer very little hope of this.

This is perhaps the only one of the *Black Paintings* which is downright satirical. Neither the toady nor the old biddies around him or Holy Herberts in the procession would frighten anybody but rather raise a grin. This, and the artist's attitude to his subjects, could well be due to the signal fact that precisely during the time of its painting, the Inquisition had at last been abolished never to rise again, not even under a restored absolutism, not even as a consequence of the many pressures brought upon Ferdinand VII to set it up and on its way again.

As even the ecclesiastic authorities confessed, the Inquisition had been as much a political as a religious institution and its baleful influence had done much to

Cat. 755 (detail)

shape Spain's cultural life. Goya himself had come under its scrutiny on various occasions, the first time for his *Caprichos* ("Fancies"), a series of engravings, and then again, after the War of Independence against the French, when he was identified as he who had painted the *Majas* belonging to Manuel Godoy which were held to be obscene works. The demise of this institucion was surely met with relief by then aging painter and this work captures his wry glee at the welcome event.

The four upper room paintings so far described have in common a more or less everyday subject matter and could be understood as scenes from Spanish life. The same could never be said of the remaining three whose meaning has given rise to a host of different and wildly conflicting readings. All three works are imbued with that silence that also permeates some of the *Disparates* ("Absurdities") engraved by the artist during the same period.

The Fates is the most accessible of the three if such a word could properly be applied to any of them. Goya draws upon three mythological figures: Clotho, Lachesis and Atropos, Daughters of Night, who grant Man both Good and Evil and harry his sins and even those of the gods. Hesiod in his *Theogony* tells us that these merciless deities never slacken in the chase until they visit their harsh punishment upon all those that have committed crimes.

There are four figures in Goya's composition here, the three goddesses themselves and a bound (?) man that they are carrying off. The artists has made short shrift of the traditional iconographic elements proper to the Fates. Clotho holds a human figure – a doll, an ex-voto of the body? – rather than her conventional distaff or spinning wheel; Lachesis does not tease out her thread of Life but rather peers at what might be a mirror or maybe it is through a quizzing glass while Atropos who put the final shears to the thread of Life is but equipped here with scissors. The man stares out at us devoid of all initiative.

If its theme is important to any understanding of the piece, as important are the elements that Goya has added to the tale. First among these must stand his having dismissed all trace of the heroically sublime or mythological. The Fates are great gods and are shown as

Cat. 757 (detail)

such in traditional written or plastic iconography. But not here, where their faces are deformed and brutal, especially Clotho's, so much so that their sex must be a given. Goya's vision of these "divine" daughters of Old Night has as little to do with the ideal nobility of Neoclassicism as it does with the sentimentalized terror of most romantic creations. If anything leaps out from his figures, it is the sordid brutality that he has seen in them. Other european artists of the period made a try at representing the gods of Night but only Goya dared to see them in this way, tossing aside everything positive, other-worldly or ideal that the notion "divine" usually urges on the artist.

And this is not the only thing that seizes the attention of the spectator, for another must be the nocturnal landscape in which the action is set. Its moonlit beauty with its silvers and golds, the luminous sky, its trees and bushes in deep shadow, the angular handling with which its working space is manipulated are all hallmarks of Goya's mastercraftsmanship. The overall effect is that of a dream, and, being dream-like, all here answers to the demands of that state. The contrast between this silent landscape and the presences and character of the Fates, the doll-like profile of he who is being borne off through the air are the elements that work the expressive effect here.

Goya had worked at nocturnal landscapes before and these recall this one, for instance in his *Caprichos* ("Fancies"), where night flying witches are shown, the same holds for the *Disparates* ("Absurdities"), where the dream-like element is as overpowering as in *Atropos* itself. Notwithstanding, a painting in oils on this scale offers much more scope than any drawing or engraving ever could, especially when it comes to the treatment given to moonlight.

56

Cat. 757 (detail)

Asmodea (cat. 756)
127 x 263 cm

This is the most hermetic of all the *Black Paintings*. Its title comes down to us via the inventory made by Goya's friend Antonio Brugada who must have had his reasons for so calling it. Whatever these were, they escape us and the work itself gives no hint of them. Asmodeus, in the masculine form, is the devil from the Book of Tobias that slew the husbands of Sarah one after the other before they could consummate their marriages. The last of them all, Tobias, on the advice of Archangel Raphael, drove off this fiend with a stench of fish and chased him off to Upper Egypt, where the Archangel bound him to Earth.

Another literary source for the painting's theme, could have been *El diablo cojuelo* ("The crippled devil") by Luis Vélez de Guevara, a narrative known to and promoted by A. R. Lesage and D. de Torres. This Asmodeus is a flying devil of popular superstition, an ability that allows him to eavesdrop on households. This source has been often forwarded.

In these and other possible sources, there is but one aspect that could tie them in with the picture and that is flying as such whereas there are many and more which disqualify them all and, above all, the fact that the title is "Asmodea" not "Asmodeus". To add to the conundrum, Goya has put soldiers firing away into the foreground right and what would seem to be an army baggage train into the background – though it is hard to tell if the first are firing on the second – both of which puts out of joint any reading of the work's images anchored upon classical sources. The modern world is very much there with its muskets, fusiliers, uniforms and carriage horses and all. Be this as it may, it would also only be right to draw attention to the fact that those in the air might be classically dressed (might be became Goya was also given to turning out modern figures in such guise). It just would not do to glide over these

60

Cat. 756 (detail)

problems and suggest a meaning that ignored them. Which does not mean that we should give up on the image which is among the most fascinating of the series with its shining sky in sharp contrast with the nocturnal luminosity of *Atropos* which, as will be remembered, stood across from this work, with its movement of flying people, the enigmatic import of those firing soldiers seen from the back, the picturesque baggage train in the background, the vasty rock crowned with buildings that one of the fliers is pointing out... I would not risk a pictorial nor historiographic commentary on this painting and yet, arguing from an association of ideas and speaking only for myself, find in it some manner of foreboding of the mood that enshroudsh some of Kafka's tales.

Things fantastic or dream-wrought rather than terrible, density and not mere portrayal, crystalline images; these are all plastic qualities in painting without which modern art would lack consistency.

A Drowning Dog (cat. 767)

131 x 79 cm

Before hazarding an interpretation, let the visitor first
give the dog's head a good look, its gaze, where its muzzle
is pointing... Apart from the ditch, these are the only
anecdotes with which to entertain the eye. The scene
could not be simpler; a dog's head is thrust forth from a
ditch, it is staring at something to the right and slightly
higher up but its gaze is at nothing – though some
historians hold that there once were fluttering birds there –
and behind this possible nothing, there is infinite space or
nothing again.

To say that this is a profoundly visual work is not,
however, to state the obvious. The few anecdotic elements
that Goya offers are by no means incomprehensible – there
is nothing puzzling about a dog's head, a ditch nor space
and yet, combined, the result is hermetic for neither dog,
ditch nor space exhibit features that allow for placing them.
Rather quite the opposite, for the dog is no more than that
– any old dog – and shorn of any attributes that could give
it any mythological standing, we have no idea of the ditch
in itself, whether it be cut into sand, clay, stone, and the
background's space could just be the painting itself. In
short, its hard to say what the painting is about because
more than anything else, it is just a painting.

Cat. 767 (detail)

An x-ray study of the work has shown that it suffered more than any of the others when being lifted on to canvas and it could be that Goya never finished it – though there is no way of knowing this for sure. Whatever the case, the work is not a jot the less effective and this to such a degree that it has become an emblematic image for modern art itself in its most obscure and anguish ridden aspects. This is not the only occasion on which Goya anticipates the inference skills proper to our own times, for they are also displayed in his *Disparates* ("Absurdities"). Be that so, at no other time does he show to such effect and with so much mastery as he does here the intractability between a figure and sheer room nor underline within a work the pure challenge and anguish inherant in existing.

The layman as much as the historian can only feel an urge to conceptualize the image, to explain it away, wrap it round with a tale: the dog is drowning in quicksand, the dog is escaping, it is coming to us, is showing its head... No one could gainsay any of these explanations but then again, none of them is as charged with expression as the painting is, not one of them clears up the cosmic dimension of the background space, nor makes clear what manner of ditch – if a ditch – the ditch is, nor even what sort of dog this dog could be. I would therefore bet that the visitor will find it hard to shake off the uneasiness and doubts that the picture gives rise to, and it is maybe this power to dog the spectator that is its real meaning. In it the *Black Paintings* as a whole reach their peak of intensity: one step further on than their anecdotal subject matter, they suggest there is a world to be looked at yet. Would it be to go too far to find our own in the dog's outlook?

Basic chronology

1819. February 27: Goya buys the *Quinta*, a country house on the banks of the River Manzanares. During the last months of the year he becomes gravely ill.

1820. On March 9: Ferdinand VII swears the 1812 Constitution. This ushers in the so-called *Trienio Liberal* ("Three Years of Liberalism"). The Inquisition is abolished on March 20. Goya swears the Constitution on April 4, before the Royal Academy.

1823. On September 17, he wills the *Quinta* to his 17 year old grandson, Mariano. As he is a minor, the deeds are handed over to Francisco Javier Goya, his father.

Invasion by the Hundred Thousand Sons of Saint Luis (French invasion under the auspices of the Holy Alliance) sent to restore absolutism. Madrid falls on May 23, Cádiz surrenders on September 30.

1824. Goya hides away in the house of Canon José Duaso y Latre. On May 30, is granted leave to take the waters at Plombières (France). After a brief stay in Paris (from June 30 to September 1) he arrives in Bordeaux.

1825. Leave to continue his waters cure is extended (January 13) and then further so for taking the baths at Bagnères (July 4).

1826. Journey to Madrid in May. Is allowed to retire on full salary (50.000 reales) on June 17.

1827. Travels to Madrid during the summer.

1828. Goya dies on April 16, attended by Leocadia Zorrilla and in the presence of Antonio Brugada and José Pío de la Molina. Antonio Brugada makes his inventory of Goya's Quinta effects.

1830. May 3, Mariano makes the *Quinta* over to his father, Francisco Javier Goya.

1832. The *Quinta* is mortgaged to Joaquín Azpiazu and let to Severiano Figueras at 8.000 reales a year. The date of this transaction is uncertain.

1854. Death of Francisco Javier Goya, March 12. December 14, The *Quinta* surveyed by the architect Manuel García for Narciso Bruguera.

1856. Death of Leocadia Zorrilla, August 6.

1857. January 2, the "Quinta" let to Santiago Ortiz who sub-lets it to Francisca Vildósola, who will be the second wife to Mariano Goya, widowed on March 14, 1859. By her he will have two daughters, Luisa and Francisca.

1859. The *Quinta* sold to Segundo Colmenares in early June.

1863. May 23, bankruptcy of Segundo Colmenares results in requisition of his goods and properties. On November, Luis Rodolfo Coumont buys the *Quinta* for 5.209.728 reales, perhaps commissions Laurent to photograph its paintings.

1873. The property, now owned by Ch. Saulnier, is bought by Baron Frédéric Emile d'Erlanger.

1874. F. E. d'Erlanger has Salvador Martínez Cubells, restorer to the Prado Museum, lift the paintings on to canvas. In this task the latter is assisted by his brothers. Enrique and Francisco.

1878. The paintings are shown in the Trocadero during the Paris World Fair.

1881. The pictures, having been bequeathed to the Spanish State, are assigned to the Prado Museum.

Basic bibliography

Angulo Íñiguez, Diego: "El *Saturno* y las *Pinturas negras* de Goya", in *Archivo Español de Arte,* XXXV, no. 138, 1962, p. 173-177.

Arnaiz, José Manuel: *Las* Pinturas negras *de Goya*, Madrid, Antiquaria, 1996.

Bozal, Valeriano: *Imagen de Goya*, Madrid, Lumen, 1983.

Bozal, Valeriano: Pinturas negras *de Goya*, Madrid, Tf. Editores, 1998.

Garrido, Carmen: "Algunas consideraciones sobre la técnica de las *Pinturas negras* de Goya", in *Boletín del Museo del Prado,* V, no. 13, 1984, p. 4-38.

Glendinning, Nigel: "The strange Translation of Goya's *Black Paintings*", in *The Burlington Magazine,* CXVII, no. 868, 1975, p. 465-479.

Glendinning, Nigel: *The Interpretation of Goya's Black Paintings,* London, Queen Mary College, 1977.

Glendinning, Nigel: "Goya's Country House en Madrid. The *Quinta del Sordo*", in *Apollo*, CXXIII, no. 288, 1986, p. 102-109.

Glendinning, Nigel: "La *Quinta del Sordo* de Goya", in *Historia 16*, XI, no. 120, 1986, p. 99-109.

Glendinning, Nigel: "Las *Pinturas negras*", in *Jornadas en torno al estado de la cuestión de los estudios sobre Goya*, Universidad Autónoma de Madrid, 4-23 October, 1992.

González de Zárate, Jesús María: *Goya de lo bello a lo sublime*, Vitoria, Instituto de Estudios Iconográficos Ephialte del Ayuntamiento de Vitoria-Gasteiz, 1990.

Licht, Fred: *Goya. The Origins of the Modern Temper in Art*, New York, Universe Books, 1979 (London, John Murray, 1980).

López Vázquez, José Manuel B.: *El programa neoplatónico de las pinturas* *de la* Quinta del Sordo, Santiago de Compostela, 1981.

Malraux, André: *Saturne (Essai sur Goya)*, Montrouge, NRF, 1950.

Moffitt, John H. F.: "Hacia el esclarecimiento de las *Pinturas negras* de Goya", in *Goya*, no. 215, 1990, p. 282-293.

Muller, Priscilla E.: *Goya's "Black" Paintings. Truth and Reason in Light and Liberty*, New York, Hispanic Society of America, 1984.

Nordström, Folke: *Goya, Saturn and Melancholy*, Almqvist & Wiksell, Stockholm, Gotemburg, Uppsala, 1962. (Spanish trans.: *Goya, Saturno y melancolía*, Madrid, Visor, 1989).

Paz, Alfredo de: *Goya: Arte e condizione umana*, Naples, Liguori Editore, 1990.

Sánchez Cantón, F. Javier: "Cómo vivía Goya", in *Archivo Español de Arte*, XVIII, no. 73, 1946.

Sánchez Cantón, F. Javier y Salas, Xavier de: *Goya y sus Pinturas negras en la Quinta del Sordo*, Barcelona, Milano, Vergara, Rizzoli, 1963.

Sebastián, S.: "Interpretación iconológica de las *Pinturas negras* de Goya", in *Goya*, no. 148-150, 1979, p. 268-277.

Torrecillas Fernández, María del Carmen: "Nueva documentación fotográfica sobre las pinturas de la *Quinta del Sordo* de Goya", en *Boletín del Museo del Prado*, VI, no. 17, 1985, p. 87-96.

Torrecillas Fernández, María del Carmen: "Las pinturas de la *Quinta del Sordo* fotografiadas por Laurent", in *Boletín del Museo del Prado*, XII, no. 31, 1992, p. 57-69.

Museo Nacional del Prado
General Information

Edificio Villanueva

Paseo del Prado, s/n. 28014 Madrid
Tel.: 91 330 29 00
Fax: 91 330 28 56
Wheelchair access available

Museum opening hours

Tuesday to Sunday and public holidays:
9:00 a.m. to 7:00 p.m.
(Last entry 30 minutes before closing. Visitors are requested to start vacating the galleries 10 minutes before closing.)
Closed on Mondays.
1 January, Good Friday, 1 May and 25 December.

Admission charges

Basic Admission: 3 €
Discounted admission (with ID): 1,5 €
- -Holders of youth cards, students' cards or international equivalents.
- -Cultural and educational groups (by prior arrangement).
- -Members of national or international museum associations.

Free admission (with ID):
- -Visitors under 18.
- -Visitors over 65, pensioners, registered disabled.
- -Unemployed.
- -Members of the Fundación Amigos del Museo del Prado.
- -Cultural and educational volunteers (by prior arrangement).

Free admission for all:
- -Sundays from 9 a.m. to 7:00 p.m.
- -18 May (International Museums Day).
- -12 October (National Holiday).
- -6 December (Constitution Day).

Cafeteria
Tueday to Sunday and public holidays from 9:00 a.m. to 6:20 p.m. 24 and 31 December from 9:00 a.m. to 1:20 p.m.

Restaurant
Tueday to Sunday and public holidays from 11:30 a.m. to 4:00 p.m.

Shops
Tueday to Sunday and public holidays from 9:00 a.m. to 6:30 p.m. 24 and 31 December from 9:00 a.m. to 1:30 p.m.

How to get there
Metro: Atocha, Banco and Retiro stations.
Bus: Numbers 9, 10, 14, 19, 27, 34, 37, 45.
From the airport: Airport shuttle bus to Plaza de Colón, then bus no. 27.

Fundación Amigos del Museo del Prado
General Information

Museo del Prado c/ Ruiz de Alarcón, 21-bajo. 28014 Madrid
Tel.: 91 420 20 46
Fax.: 91 429 50 20
E-mail: info@amigosmuseoprado.org
Internet: www.amigosmuseoprado.org
Office hours:
Monday to Friday, from 9:30 a.m. to 2:30 p.m.